Collection of Stories and Fables with Morals and Values

Julia Ardiles de Espinoza

Uncle Rabbit
Collection of Stories and Fables
with Morals and Values

Copyright © 2019 Julia Ardiles de Espinoza
First Edition, April 2012

Written by:
Julia Ardiles de Espinoza

Graphic Design and Illustration:
Grafi-K Comunicación and Diseño S.A.C.

ISBN 978-0-578-49868-3 (paperback)

Printed in the United States of America

All rights reserved. No part of this publication may be reproduced without the prior permission of the publisher.

Dear Reader:

It is my joy to know that you're about to read a collection of entertaining, hilarious, and exotic fables. These beautiful stories made up great part of my childhood.

My daddy Alejandro Ardiles Caja used to tell us these stories every night. I remember my family would cuddle up to listen to my dad narrate these enriching fables.

The best part of these stories is that each fable has a lesson. These lessons have much wisdom! Enjoy!

May the Lord Jesus Christ receive all the glory!

Julia Ardiles de Espinoza

 **100%** of proceeds will go to panperu.org

Pan Peru is a 501(c)3 nonprofit organization that empowers women, children, and the environment by building multimedia libraries, executing reforestation programs, and empowering underserved females to become entrepreneurs. Pan Peru was founded in 2004 by engineer Julia Ardiles de Espinoza with the vision to foster and promote education in one of the least developed nations of Latin America.

www.panperu.org

Introduction

This is just one of the stories I have collected that is based on either an anonymous folktale or is from a known storyteller and fabulist of the world. Some of the stories I collect are attributed to Aesop, to the Frenchman Jean de la Fontaine, or to the Spanish writer Felix Maria Samaniego.

With some of them, like "The Lion and the Little Mouse" and "The Lion in Love," we can find fables attributed to Aesop, as adapted by Samaniego. "The Dog and the Wolf" is an adaptation of a story by La Fontaine, and the "Marquis of Carabas" is an adaptation of "Puss in Boots," an anonymous European folk tale collected by Charles Perrault in 1697.

Uncle Rabbit

One morning, a limber-legged, popular, and playful rabbit called Uncle Rabbit organized a meeting to elect the new king of the jungle.

"Me, me, me!" yelled the elephant. "I'm the heaviest and with a single stomp (BOOM!), I can shake the earth and bring order to the kingdom."

"Me, me!" screamed the giraffe. "Because I'm the tallest, and when I stretch my neck I can see what happens in the entire jungle in a matter of seconds."

"Me, me!" proclaimed the tiger. "Because I'm the fastest and if there is any problem anywhere, I can get there immediately."

"Me...!" roared the lion. "I'm the bravest and with my roar (Grrrrrrrr!), I can make all the animals tremble and freak out."

The following animals signed up for the election: the hippo, crocodile, gazelle, turtle, monkey, mole, and many more. Each boasted and then showed off their best traits. At the end of the election, there was a tie between the tiger and the lion. However, one final vote was missing–Uncle Rabbit's. Even though he had organized the meeting–knocking on every door and jumping from branch to branch–he didn't show up at the election.

In order to decide the winner, the kingdom needed Uncle Rabbit's vote as soon as possible.

The tiger was very lazy and didn't want to get up from his spot. Meanwhile, the lion went looking for Uncle Rabbit with the intention of earning his vote to win the election.

After a long run, the lion found the rabbit peacefully sleeping. Uncle Rabbit was taking advantage of the calm sunset.

"We need you, Uncle Rabbit!" yelled the lion. "You need to decide between the tiger and me, who will be the next king of the jungle…"

Uncle Rabbit stretched, polished and sharpened his big teeth, picked up something for the road, and climbed onto the lion's back, ready to cast his vote.

While the lion was rushing through the jungle to impress Uncle Rabbit, the clever rabbit was planning his own campaign to become the king of the jungle.

At last, the lion arrived at the meeting point, sweaty and with sore muscles. With a very weak and tired voice, the lion said:

"I found Uncle Rabbit. He was sleeping."

Instead of voting, Uncle Rabbit declared:

"Neither the tiger, who did not even move because he's lazy, nor the lion, who's old and easily tired, deserve to be the king of the jungle. I should be the king because I am important. I am irreplaceable. You need me. Otherwise, you wouldn't have spent hours searching for me."

All of the animals laughed at Uncle Rabbit's proposal. However, they decided to hold a new election—this time between the lion, for being the strongest, and Uncle Rabbit, for being the boldest. They agreed to let the rabbit rule for a month.

The next day, there were huge signs throughout the jungle: in the trees, bushes, and riversides. It was the first day of Uncle Rabbit's rule and the animals could see the signs. They said: all animals should sow and eat carrots 24/7, since vitamin A is great for your vision.

The animals finally elected Uncle Rabbit as the king, because he exceeded their expectations. Without a doubt, Uncle Rabbit's qualities surpassed the qualities of his rival. During Uncle Rabbit's rule, the vision of the animals improved greatly thanks to his carrot policy.

The Story's Lesson:
Vegetables are healthy for you!
Even Uncle Rabbit recommends it!

The Lovestruck Lion

Once upon a time, a beautiful peasant girl was walking in the countryside when she heard someone whistle: Fiu, fiu, fiu! She turned—curious to see who was wooing her—and saw a lion. The pretty girl was quite surprised. She was speechless and fearful. Immediately, she tried to hide her fear with a smile.

Since that day, the lion pursued the girl with his charming whistles, sweet words, and romantic poems—the lion even tried singing opera to her. He begged her to marry him, promising her that she would be the queen of the jungle.

The beautiful girl didn't want to marry the lion. The worst part was that she didn't know how to tell that to the lion. She didn't even know how to avoid him. One day, she said:

"But lion, to marry me, you must first request my father's permission..."

The devoted lion immediately went to ask the father for the girl's hand in marriage. Calmly, the father said:

"I will happily grant you my daughter's hand. She will have the honor of marrying you, Your Majesty, but only on one condition: you must cut off your nails and pull out your teeth because they scare her. My precious daughter panics when she sees your large nails and sharp teeth."

Without thinking twice, the lion—who was madly in love—got his nails and teeth removed.

Afterwards, the lion went back with great enthusiasm to ask for the hand of the beautiful peasant. This time, the girl's father—seeing no claws and no teeth—kicked him out of the house with a massive karate kick.

The Story's Lesson:
Love may be blind, but not stupid.

The Limp Little Donkey

Once upon a time, a little donkey was walking through a field. All of a sudden, he stepped on a thorn bush. This accident left him with a limp...

Since then, anyone could recognize the little donkey thanks to the noise he made when he limped: Tin, tipin, tin, tipin. Tin, tipin.

After walking for several hours in a huge amount of pain, the donkey decided to take a power nap. Out of nowhere, a fierce wolf appeared with a greedy appetite.

As soon as the donkey saw him, he thought:

"Snap! Double snap! This wolf is going to devour me in two seconds. I must come up with a plan to avoid him... Ah! I know..." The little donkey had a fantastic plan.

"Hey donkey, I'm hungry and you'll be my appetizer!" exclaimed the wolf.

The limp little donkey replied:

"Sir Wolf, before I die, please grant me a final wish. I stepped on a thorn and I'm in pain. Since you look like an outstanding doctor, could you operate on me so that I can die without pain?"

The wolf felt praised by what the donkey said. He thought, "Oh, I look like a doctor! I must be very handsome and elegant!"
So the wolf proudly replied:
"Of course, I'll operate on you. Raise your leg."

As soon as the wolf had finished speaking, the limp little donkey raised his leg and kicked the wolf. It was such a strong kick that the donkey broke the wolf's jaw, teeth, and chin.

The wolf lay on the ground whining. In a matter of seconds, the violent animal turned into a powerless predator. The donkey walked away braying and giggling.

The Story's Lesson:
Be careful when a stranger praises you.

The Marquis of Carabas

Once upon a time, there was a peasant who had three sons. One day, feeling that his strength had run out and that he was about to die, he called for his sons and told them:

"Before I die, I want to distribute among you the few things that I have."

To the eldest son he gave a donkey, to the middle son a mill, and to the last son a cat.

The eldest son was extremely happy, because the donkey was a source of money: he could start a transportation business. The middle son was also excited because the mill could grind the beans everyone needed. The last son, however, was upset. With a gloomy attitude he questioned, "How can I make money with a cat? On the contrary, it's going to create more expenses."

The stressed young man was about to leave the cat when he heard a voice say:

"Meow! Master don't worry, I'll make you a millionaire. Just buy me a red silk cape, a hat with feathers, and a pair of boots with golden buckles."

The young man was shocked to hear the cat talking and thought, "This cat must be special. It's amazing that he can speak." Persuaded by the cat, the young man bought everything the cat asked for.

He took the cat to the tailor to customize its coat, then to the shoemaker to make the boots and the hat. "I'm spending all my money and I hope it's not in vain," he thought.

"Meow! Master, trust me. I will make you very, very rich," promised the cat.

Every morning, the cat left the house of his master carrying an empty bag. He went to the forest to fill the little bag with carrots, lettuce, beans, etc. Then he hid among the plants and waited until something fell into his trap: a rabbit, partridge, or pigeon. Then he quickly tied the bag and returned to the house to dress up—putting on his elegant coat, hat, and boots with the golden buckles—to go to the royal palace.

The cat boastfully announced to all the guards, footmen, and the king that he was sent by the Marquis of Carabas. The cat handed the bag to the king with great respect, stating:

"Your Majesty, please receive this humble gift from my master, the Marquis of Carabas."

The king admired the cat's elegant speech, and rewarded him with a small bag of golden coins. Then, the cat gave his master the coins, making him very happy.

The cat boldly continued to deliver different gifts to the king from his master, the Marquis of Carabas. Eventually, the king became very curious as to who was sending him so many gifts. So one day, the king waited for the cat and asked:

"Who is the Marquis of Carabas?"

The cat, without blinking, replied:

"He is a noble, pure, and admirable knight. He is an outstandingly handsome and wealthy master who lives in your kingdom. He thinks you are a wise and impressive king."

"I want to meet him," said the king. "I have a young daughter and I want her to marry him next summer."

During one of his trips to the palace, the cat overheard the king telling his court: "let's go to a pond in the countryside tomorrow!"

"Aha!" exclaimed the cat as he combed his whiskers, brewing a plan.

The next day, the cat persuaded his master to take a bath in the pond so that he could run into the king's daughter. The young man was hesitant to go. He felt embarrassed, but the cat convinced him by saying:

"Just follow my orders and you will see."

As a result, both of them, went to the pond. While the man was taking a bath, the cat hid in the bushes and waited for the arrival of the royal court.

When the royal guards approached the pond, the cat exclaimed:

"Help! Thieves assaulted my master, the Marquis of Carabas!"

Immediately, the king ordered everyone to stop and help the Marquis. The king sent guards to get silk clothes for the Marquis. The youngster transformed into a very elegant and handsome man thanks to the royal clothing. The king invited him into the royal carriage. As soon as the attractive Marquis hopped in, the princess fell in love with him. Both of them were smiling and flirting with each other.

Extending his hand, the king said:

"I am pleased to meet you, Marquis of Carabas. Thank you very much for your countless gifts. I am truly honored to have you with us. Certainly, I would love to visit your land."

The Marquis nodded, but he was worried. At that moment, the cat said:

"Your Majesty, it will be an honor to show you the wonderful properties of my master. I will go ahead to prepare the way and guide the carriage."

Then the cat began to run down the path. Along the way, the cat found farmers who were harvesting wheat fields, cornfields, apples, grapes, and carrots. During those times, an abusive, evil one-eyed ogre owned all of the lands. The clever cat asked the farmers:

"Do you want to be free from the ogre forever?"
"Yes!" the farmers responded as one.
"Ok! So, when the royal carriage comes and the king asks—'Who's the owner of these lands?'—you have to respond with respect and say in a loud voice: 'The Marquis of Carabas.' Sound good?"
"Yes!"

And when the king saw the wheat fields, cornfields, and grape vines, he asked the peasants:

"Hello, farmers. Who owns this land?"

"The Marquis of Carabas," they all answered.

The king was impressed by the wealth of the Marquis of Carabas. As a result, the princess fell more in love with him.

At the end of the path, the cat went to a crystal palace. There, he saw the evil one-eyed ogre.

"Grrr! How dare you come to my palace without my permission?" shouted the ogre. "Don't you know that I can turn into any animal and devour you?"

At that moment, the ogre transformed into a fierce lion. "Grrrrrr!" And he almost devoured the cat except that the cat, thanks to its fast reflexes, saved itself by climbing onto the roof.

When the ogre turned back to normal, the cat jumped down from the roof and challenged the ogre, saying:

"I admire your powers, Sir Ogre, but I doubt you can become a small animal."

"Like what?" asked the ogre.

"Like a little mouse!"

"Of course I can! Look!"

Without thinking twice, the ogre turned into a small mouse. At that moment, the cat ate him, freeing everyone from the evil ogre forever. Then the cat ran victoriously to meet the king and his court. With a joyful voice, he said:

"Welcome to the luxurious palace of my master, the Marquis of Carabas!"

The Marquis was intrigued because he didn't own any sort of palace. But the cat winked at his master, letting him know that everything would be all right.

The king gladly granted his daughter's hand to the Marquis of Carabas.

They got married and lived happily ever after.

THE STORY'S LESSON:
With much ingenuity, intelligence, and might, one can turn a peasant into a knight.

The Little Pig and the Baby Horse

The Little Pig and the Baby Horse

Don Jacinto was a well-known farmer. He owned many acres of land and all kinds of livestock. One of Don Jacinto's favorite animals was a well-bred foal that he intended to use as the stallion for his mares.

One morning, Gerardo—the boy responsible for feeding and taking care of the horses—noticed that his master's favorite horse couldn't walk. Gerardo immediately informed Don Jacinto.

Don Jacinto went out with his workers to find the most talented local vets to cure the baby horse.

After a few hours, three veterinarians came to the farm. They carefully examined the horse. All three gave the same answer:

"The horse is very ill. He won't recover. He can't be cured because he has a terminal disease. It's better to sacrifice him."

Don Jacinto was very sad when he heard the news.

"What's going on? This can't be happening!" he said. "I can't lose my foal." So he called other vets. Don Jacinto brought in the most renowned vets in the region by offering acres of land to whoever could cure his horse.

In a matter of hours, many veterinarians arrived at the farm. After examining the animal, they concluded: "This horse can't be cured."

Suddenly, an old veterinarian who lived in a nearby village carefully examined the sick horse. He said:

"I have the solution! I'm experimenting with a powerful, new medicine. We'll give him three injections—one per day. If the horse doesn't get up on the third day, we'll have to sacrifice him."

Don Jacinto accepted the offer. He trusted the vet because he had many years of experience. But, most importantly, he offered hope.

While Don Jacinto was talking to the experienced vet, a little pig was listening. He heard the plan to kill the horse if he couldn't get up on the third day.

In a matter of minutes, the pig warned the other animals of what would happen on the third day if the foal couldn't stand. All of the animals promised to help in any way possible, from massaging his neck to singing opera.

The pig approached the horse and said, "Little horse, don't worry. We promise to help you."

When they gave him the first injection, the horse didn't walk. The second day brought the same result. That night, the little pig pledged to the other animals that he would serve as support for the horse and help him walk the next day.

On the last day, after he received the third injection, all of the animals—large and small—pulled the horse. They made him stand on his feet and walk. When Don Jacinto saw his beloved horse had passed the test, he felt extremely happy and started to cry with joy.

Grateful, Don Jacinto gave the vet a huge reward and invited him to his house for lunch.

"Come to the farm on Sunday with all of your family. Let me treat you to a delicious banquet. I'll kill my pig to create a great meal for your family. I'm so blessed to know you!"

The horse heard Don Jacinto's offer and waited until Saturday night to quietly wake up the pig.

"Your life is in danger. Get on my back and let's run away," he whispered to his friend.

The baby horse and the little pig escaped from the farm and never returned.

THE STORY'S LESSON:
Sincere friendships can bring us endless blessings such as loyalty, trust, and love.

The Lion and the Little Mouse

One summer evening in the jungle, after eating gazelles, Mr. Lion decided to take a nap. Fatigued by the hunting session, he lay down under a tree.

Out of nowhere, three mice started jumping on the lion's belly. These mice walked on top of the lion's back and started to play around. The smallest mouse bit the lion's hair.

The lion thought it was a fly and wagged his tail to scare it away. However, the lion failed to frighten the animal. The mouse continued playing around, disturbing the lion's dream.

The mouse was so hyper that he woke up the lion. When the lion saw the little mouse, he exclaimed:

"Gggrrr...! How dare you interrupt my sleep?! Don't you realize that I can eat you in a bite? I'm super strong. Why are you playing with my hair?

I can easily kill you!"

Thankfully, the lion forgave the mouse because he felt sorry to see a poor mouse asking for forgiveness with his hands pressed together in prayer.

"Thank you so much, Mr. Lion, for sparing my life," said the little mouse. "I didn't mean to disturb your sleep. But your beautiful hair caught my attention, and I couldn't stop playing with it. Thank you. Someday I will repay you the favor. I owe you a big one!"

Impressed by his words, the lion mocked the mouse with a big smile:

"How in the world will you repay me? You're not even as large as one of my claws! Get out of here and let me finish dreaming of beautiful pineapples and mangos."

Several months later, the three mice were playing in the jungle when they heard a big

animal groaning. Out of curiosity, they decided to find out what was going on... surprise! A lion was trapped in a net. The poor animal had fallen into a hunter's trap.

The youngest mouse immediately recognized the lion who had spared his life. Calmly, he said:

"Don't worry, your Majesty. My brothers and I will help you in the blink of an eye."

Carefully and quickly, the mice gnawed the ropes with their sharp tiny teeth: chuck, chuck, chuck! They worked silently to avoid any problems with the hunters. In less than a minute, Mr. Lion was free again and ready to reclaim his kingdom. The lion was very impressed by the mice's speed and their quick ability to solve the problem.

The lion was also embarrassed, and he learned to never underestimate the little mouse. After all, his life had been saved because he had shown the mouse mercy. The lion thanked his rescuers and immediately went to take care of the hunters. Mr. Lion gave a loud roar ("Gggrrrr!") that drove the hunters away.

In the end, the joyful little mice continued to play their games in the mighty jungle.

The Lucky Farmer

Once upon a time, there was a king who was fair and generous to his people. Everyone lived happily. Farmers worked their lands and fed their livestock. Many honest and trustworthy merchants lived in this community. However, like everywhere in the world, there was a jealous neighbor who always complained.

During harvest season, Virgilio—a kindhearted and humble peasant—was surprised when he saw a giant potato. This potato was different from the rest of the potatoes he reaped. It was still connected to the ground. The peasant dug out tons of mud and still couldn't remove the potato, so he asked his neighbors for help.

The humble farmer thanked the earth for providing such a giant potato. With a grateful heart, he also thanked his neighbors for their help. Then, he thought: "What should I do with this massive potato?" He received thousands of suggestions from his neighbors, even from the envious farmer who wanted the potato for himself.

Virgilio was still wondering what to do with the giant potato. "If I eat it, will it taste like the other potatoes? If I sell it, I'll spend the money in no time at all," he thought. Finally, he decided to give it to the king of the province. He put the potato on a wheelbarrow and went to the castle where King Philip lived.

When the palace guards realized that someone was bringing a gift, they quickly opened the doors. The king immediately paid attention to Virgilio, not only because Virgilio brought a gift, but also because he knew of his trustworthiness. As soon as Virgilio approached the royal living room, the king said:

"Perhaps you're a magician. How did you harvest a giant potato?"

The farmer respectfully answered, "I'm just a humble peasant who comes to bring Your Majesty my best harvest of all time."

The king joyfully listened to Virgilio and gladly accepted the gift, knowing that the farmer had a pure and genuine heart.

"Thank you for the kind gift! But you won't go back empty-handed," said the king.

The king ordered the guards to fill the farmer's wheelbarrow with a variety of sweets and chocolates. He also handed the farmer a bag full of golden coins.

When Virgilio returned to the farm, his neighbors asked him about his royal visit to the palace. He briefly told them about his experience. He also shared with them the delights the king had offered him and showed them the golden coins.

Later on, the jealous neighbor filled a wheelbarrow with his best harvest: apples, pears, giant grapes, juicy mangos, and delicious oranges. With great hopes of receiving a gift in return, the envious neighbor went to the palace to see the king. He imagined that his reward would be better than Virgilio's.

King Philip received him and, after listening to him, became aware of his envy and desire for success. The king appreciated the gesture and gave the envious neighbor Virgilio's giant potato in return.

Furious, the jealous neighbor returned to the farm with much difficulty as he pushed the potato in his wheelbarrow.

THE STORY'S LESSON:
Jealousy can lead you to make poor decisions.

The Dog and the Wolf

Once upon a time, there was a very hungry wolf in the forest. The wolf was so hungry that his stomach was growling. He wandered from one side to the other

with the hope that he would find something to eat before he starved to death.

Suddenly, he saw a house with a smoky chimney a short distance away. The wolf got super excited! Nevertheless, he rubbed his eyes to make sure he wasn't seeing things. Fortunately, he was not daydreaming. He clearly saw the smoke coming out of the chimney.

The wolf started to approach the house with extreme caution. Right away, he noticed that the house seemed abandoned: no signs of life, zero noise, and closed doors. The wolf was hoping that he might find food to satisfy his hunger. At the same time, however, the wolf was afraid the owners had a weapon that could kill him.

The wolf got to the door of the abandoned house. Clearly, the smoke was there. "Someone has to live here," he said.

He decided to look through the keyhole, and he saw a huge dog licking the ground next to a hot soup with steamed sweet potatoes and carrots. The dog seemed very calm and well-fed. Without a doubt, the dog was not starving like the wolf.

Immediately, the wolf started to plan: "First, I will devour the food and then the dog. But how do I enter if everything is closed?"

The wolf walked around the house several times as he tried to find a way to enter. Unfortunately, he failed to find one. He got so tired and upset that he almost fainted. Finally, he decided to break into the house through the window. "But if I don't have the strength to walk around the house,

how can I have the energy to jump up and break the window?" he thought. Also, he noticed that he could get stuck in the window due to its small size.

"I have a better idea!" the wolf exclaimed. "I'll convince the dog to open the door by bragging about how beautiful it is to live freely in the field without an owner."

He then started to persuade the dog through the keyhole. He described the joy he had as a free animal who walked freely through the forest and knew hundreds of beautiful places:

"Hey, dog! You'll have the same life if you open the door and let me in. I'll tell you all of my adventures. And I'll take you to all of these wonderful places where you'll have unlimited bones to chew on."

The dog listened to him, and he started to approach the door to unlock it. Then, all of a sudden, the dog stopped. The dog was less than a foot away from the door, but he couldn't reach it. He was tied to a leash. The wolf shouted impatiently:

"Dog, hurry up! Open the door, buddy! You can do it! You're so close!"

The wolf looked through the keyhole and saw the poor dog unsuccessfully trying to reach the door. He also noticed a horrible bruise on the dog's neck—a result from the restraining leash.

Immediately, the wolf considered the situation and concluded: "If my freedom is going to be in danger, I'd rather be free—even if I am hungry." As a result, the wolf left.

The Story's Lesson:
Freedom comes with a price.
Learn to appreciate your freedom.

The Salt, the Sponges and the Donkey

The Salt, the Sponges and the Donkey

Once upon a time, there was a farmer who had a herd of donkeys and a pair of horses.

One day, he had to take a bag of salt and two giant bags of sponges to a faraway village to fill a mattress.

The mule driver was deceived by the package sizes. He put the salt—the smaller packet—on the donkey's back and the larger load of sponges on one of the horses. Then he mounted his horse and started his trip.

Halfway through the journey, the donkey complained about his bad luck. He told the horse:

"It's not fair that I have the heaviest burden. You're bigger than me and you have the lighter bag."

They walked a long way and the donkey began to feel tired. He suggested switching bags with the horse in order to get some rest. Unfortunately, the horse refused:

"Because you're a donkey, you will always carry the heaviest load. I'm a well-bred horse and will never carry the heaviest load."

The horse had hardly finished talking when they got to a river. Surprisingly, the river was very deep. The master checked the depth with his horse and said: "My animals are used to swimming and will easily cross this river."

And so they did. The animals began to swim, and their loads got wet.

The donkey crossed easily. His load became lighter, as the salt dissolved in the water. The horse, however, crossed with greater effort because the sponges absorbed the water and became heavier.

Sadly, the donkey almost fainted due to the heat and intense labor. When the master saw this, he took the load of salt and the exhausted donkey, and added both of them to the horse's load.

So, the horse who didn't want to help the donkey ended up carrying the sponges, the salt, and the tired donkey.

THE STORY'S LESSON:
Do not be selfish.

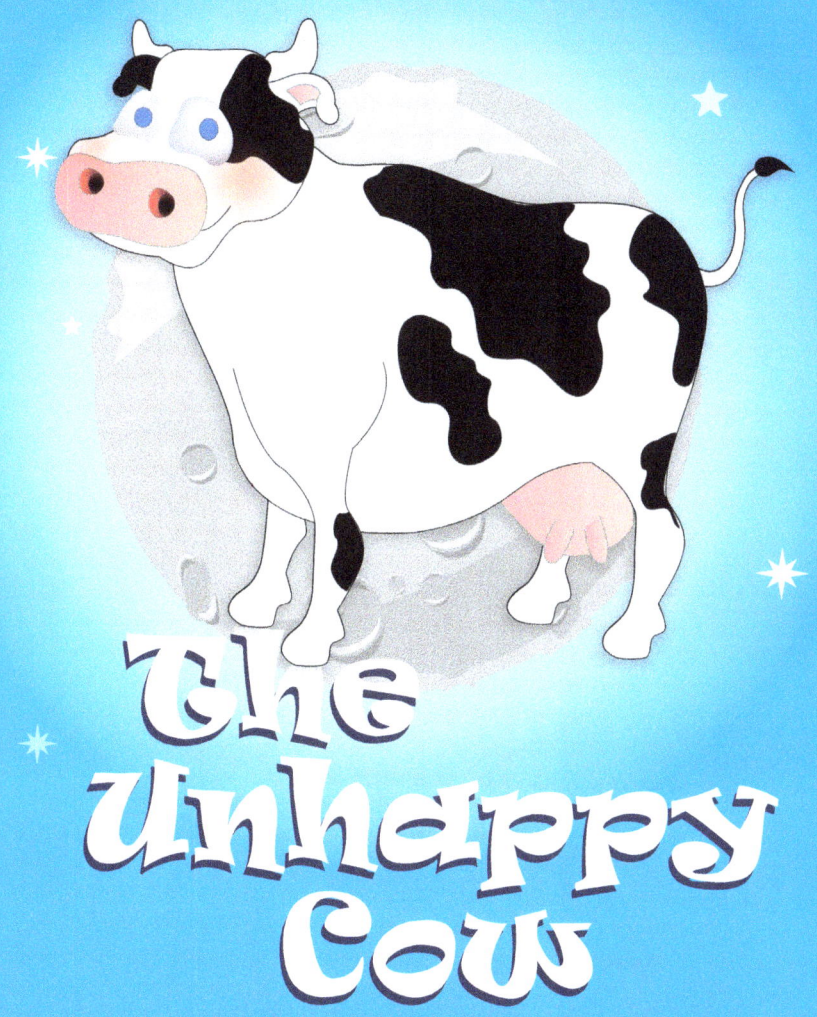

The Unhappy Cow

Once upon a time, there was a cow who gave plenty of milk and the whole family was very happy. But the cow was not happy. Whenever the opportunity came, she told the animals why she was so unhappy.

She said it bothered her that she had been born with two colors. She wanted to be white as the snow or black as coal, not both black and white.

Everyone heard about her unhappiness from sunrise to sunset. The cow constantly whined and this annoyed the other animals. This is why they called her Unhappy.

One day, all of the animals secretly agreed to talk with the boy who cared for Unhappy.

During this brief meeting, the animals asked the boy for a brush and black paint. Since the rooster and the horse always woke up earlier than the cow, the animals decided that the rooster and the horse would paint Unhappy's body black.

And so they did. One early morning, with the brush, black paint, and a bit of black shoe polish, they painted Unhappy entirely black.

When Unhappy woke up, she noticed that her dream had come true. Now she was a happy cow. Unhappy joyfully wagged her tail with enthusiasm. She stopped being an angry cow who complained and annoyed the rest of the animals.

One night, the cloudy sky started to pour rain. The animal owners were concerned about the livestock and gathered them under a shelter. Unfortunately, the owners couldn't find Unhappy because she blended in with the black clouds.

Unhappy spent the entire night, shivering by herself. Eventually, the rain washed away the paint, revealing her natural colors.

The animals feared Unhappy would start whining again. But, to everyone's surprise, Unhappy didn't complain. She wasn't even upset! She even joked about the black paint that no longer coated her body.

Unhappy learned that being joyful depends on having a positive attitude toward life, regardless of the challenges and problems one faces.

THE STORY'S LESSON
Always be happy and grateful
for what God has given you.

www.ingramcontent.com/pod-product-compliance
Lightning Source LLC
Chambersburg PA
CBHW062023290426
44108CB00024B/2759